DEADLY SNAKES

DEADLY COBRAS

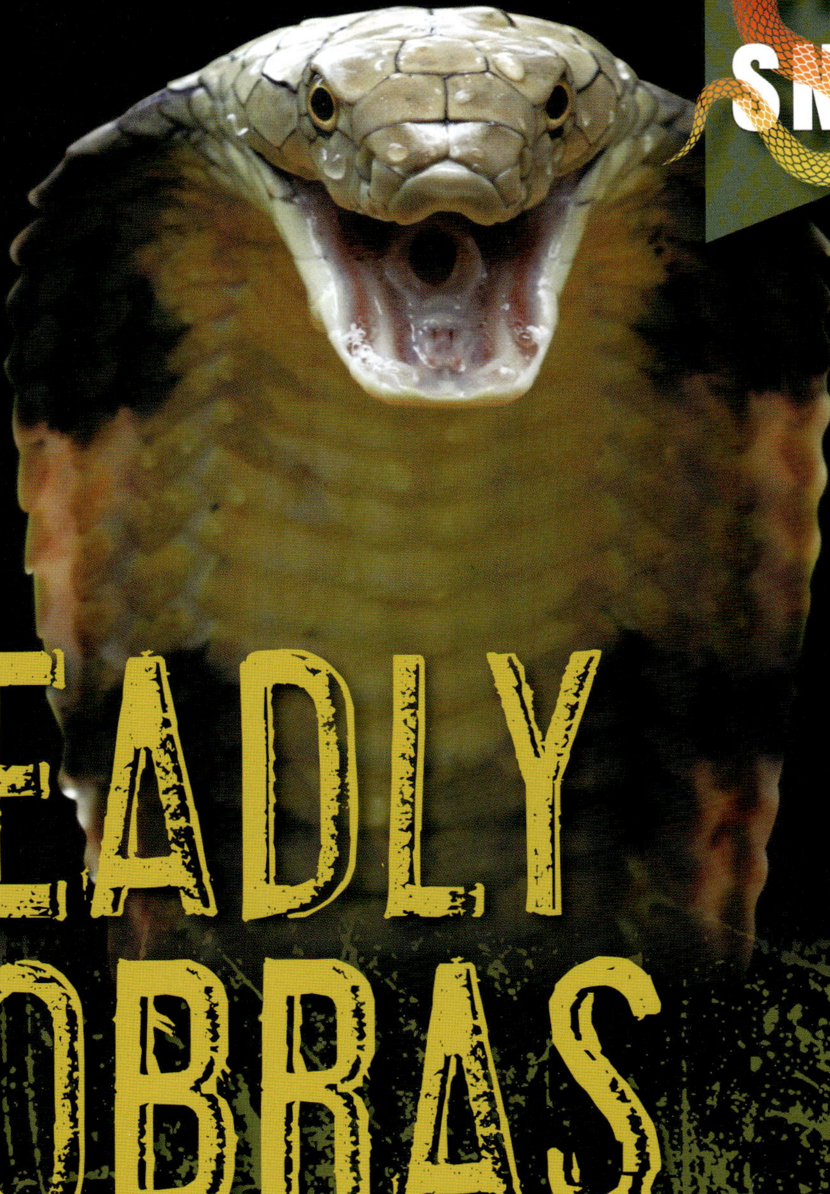

MONIKA DAVIES

Please visit our website, www.garethstevens.com. For a free color catalog of all our high-quality books, call toll free 1-800-542-2595 or fax 1-877-542-2596.

Library of Congress Cataloging-in-Publication Data
Names: Davies, Monika, author.
Title: Deadly cobras / Monika Davies.
Description: New York : Gareth Stevens Publishing, [2023] | Series: Deadly snakes | Includes index.
Identifiers: LCCN 2021050755 (print) | LCCN 2021050756 (ebook) | ISBN 9781538279762 (set) | ISBN 9781538279779 (library binding) | ISBN 9781538279755 (paperback) | ISBN 9781538279786 (ebook)
Subjects: LCSH: Cobras–Juvenile literature. | Poisonous snakes–Juvenile literature.
Classification: LCC QL666.O64 D383 2023 (print) | LCC QL666.O64 (ebook) | DDC 597.96/42–dc23/eng/20211201
LC record available at https://lccn.loc.gov/2021050755
LC ebook record available at https://lccn.loc.gov/2021050756

First Edition

Portions of this work were originally authored by Dennis Rudenko and published as *Cobras*. All new material this edition authored by Monika Davies.

Published in 2023 by
Gareth Stevens Publishing
29 E. 21st Street
New York, NY 10010

Designer: Sheryl Kober
Editor: Monika Davies

Photo credits: Cover, pp. 1, 5 Kurit afshen/Shutterstock.com; cover (snake illustration) vinap/Shutterstock.com; cover, pp. 1–24 (background texture) Anna Timoshenko/Shutterstock.com; pp. 1–24 (snakeskin) Natalliya85/Shutterstock.com; pp. 1–24 (halftone texture) MPFphotography/Shutterstock.com; pp. 13, 11, 16 (snake illustration) vinap/Shutterstock.com; pp. 4,7, 8, 15, 19, 20 (fatal facts texture) Pakhnyushchy/Shutterstock.com; p. 6 Roberto 33 /Shutterstock.com; p. 9 Yash2109/Shutterstock.com; p. 10 Peter Hermes Furian/Shutterstock.com; p. 12 Ton Bangkeaw/Shutterstock.com; p. 13 Martin Prochazkacz/Shutterstock.com; p. 14 Heiko Kiera/Shutterstock.com, p. 17 nil_sharma/Shutterstock.com; p. 18 Stu Porter/Shutterstock.com; p. 21 HarrisD/Shutterstock.com.

Printed in the United States of America

CPSIA compliance information: Batch #CSGS23: For further information contact Gareth Stevens, New York, New York, at 1-800-542-2595.

CONTENTS

Words in the glossary appear in **bold** type the first time they are used in the text.

THE CHILLING COBRA

A long, hungry snake **slithers** through an Asian forest, on the hunt for its next meal. The snake's tongue flicks out to smell the air. Then, a mouse darts across the snake's path. The snake strikes, sinking its long, pointed teeth into the mouse. *Gulp!*

Meet the cobra, a deadly snake with **venom** in its bite. A big king cobra can "stand up" and be eye-to-eye with a human! But while cobras have killer senses, they're more likely to slither away than attack another predator. Let's get to know the chilling cobra better.

FATAL FACTS

Experts disagree about how many species, or kinds, of cobras there are. Depending on what you consider a cobra, there are between 20 to about 270 species of this snake across the world.

The king cobra is perhaps the best-known type of cobra, as it is often seen alongside "snake charmers." It is the longest venomous snake in the world.

Cobras can spread their hood open and rear up when they feel unsafe. This makes them look bigger and scarier.

SPY THE COBRA

It can be tricky to point out a cobra. In fact, cobras come in many colors, such as black, yellow, green, and brown. But cobras also usually have certain features. Most cobras can spread out the ribs in their neck to create a flat hood. Many also have patterns such as V shapes and stripes on their skin.

Cobras kill their **prey** with venom, which they **inject** from two long teeth called fangs. The fangs **pierce** the skin of the cobra's prey and deliver deadly venom.

FATAL FACTS

Some cobras grow to huge lengths. The forest cobra is one of the longest cobras, sometimes reaching over 8 feet (2.4 m) in length. The king cobra can grow up to 18 feet (5.5 m) long!

A COBRA'S CHILDHOOD

Most cobras start their life inside an egg. A king cobra can lay between 20 and 40 eggs at a time. It takes more than two months for babies to break out of their shells. During that time, the mother cobra guards her eggs with care.

The mother cobra makes a nest for her eggs, moving her body around to collect leaves. She then uses the leaves to cover her eggs, later lying on top of the eggs to keep them safe.

FATAL FACTS

Baby cobras have venom too! Baby cobras are just as deadly as their parents and can take care of themselves as soon as they're born.

The king cobra is the only species of snake that makes a nest for its eggs.

WHERE KING COBRAS LIVE

King cobras mainly live in southeast and southern Asia. You can spy them in parts of India, China, Indonesia, and the Philippines.

HOME LIFE

Cobras are found in many different areas of the world. Many kinds of cobras live throughout Africa and Asia. Their colors and patterns may be different depending on their **region.**

Most cobras like to live in tropical **habitats**, which are hot and wet. They can climb trees! Others like to slither along the ground in grasslands. Sometimes they sneak onto farms to hunt. Cobras can even be found swimming through the water. While they usually prefer slithering across land, cobras can swim short distances.

STEALTHY SENSES

Cobras are skilled hunters thanks to their special senses. They have good eyesight, especially at night. They have a special body part called a Jacobson's **organ** on the roof of their mouth. A cobra's tongue collects a smell and then sends it to the Jacobson's organ, which recognizes the smell.

Cobras can sense **vibrations** in the ground. This helps them know when prey or predators are nearby. Cobras can even sense changes in heat around them. Nothing can get past a cobra!

While cobras can seem like scary hunters, they only attack a person if they feel in danger. Most of the time, they like to escape and get away from people.

Hiss! The king cobra puffs and hisses to scare away predators. Its hiss is lower than that of many other snakes, and it sounds like a dog's growl!

STAY AWAY!

Most animals stay far, far away from a cobra. They don't want to get close! The cobra has also developed **defenses** that keep predators and people away.

If a cobra feels unsafe, it may raise the upper part of its body off the ground. Large cobras can tower over their enemy. The cobra spreads its neck ribs so its hood flattens out. The hood makes it look bigger to other animals. Then, the snake will hiss, a clear warning sign to stay away!

FATAL FACTS

While cobras can also try to look scary, some species will "play dead" if they want to stay away from a predator. These cobras will lie very still on the ground, waiting until the danger is gone.

WHAT'S FOR DINNER?

Cobras are far from picky eaters. They eat many different animals. In fact, they will eat almost anything they can find, catch, and swallow. Some even eat their own kind! They also eat other kinds of snakes, especially smaller ones.

Cobras most often eat mice, rats, squirrels, and rabbits. They also hunt lizards and birds, and they will eat eggs. If a cobra comes across a dead animal, it'll likely eat it as well. Cobras take a long time to **digest** their food. This means they can go weeks or even months without eating.

Cobras will hunt for many years. They usually live to be around 20 years old in the wild.

There are spitting cobras that can spray venom from their fangs. If a spitting cobra is in danger, it can "spit" its venom up to 6.5 feet (2 m) away!

VENOMOUS HUNTERS

Cobras often search for food at dawn or dusk. When they find a meal, they strike very quickly to take their prey by surprise. Cobras deliver a venomous bite with their sharp fangs.

A bite from a cobra can be enough to kill a large animal, such as an elephant. While their venom isn't as strong as that of some snakes, cobras deliver a large amount of venom in each bite. A king cobra's bite has enough venom to kill 20 people!

FATAL FACTS

Most animals die if they are bitten by a cobra. However, if a person is bitten, they can take a medicine called antivenin (also spelled antivenom). This stops the effects of venom.

CARING FOR COBRAS

Cobras are skilled hunters with deadly instincts. Few animals are safe from them. However, cobras still have predators they'd like to avoid.

People are perhaps the greatest danger to cobras. In Southeast Asia, large parts of forests have been cut down, destroying a home for king cobras. Many cobras are hunted for their skin or for use as medicine. While cobras are not quite an **endangered** species, they're vulnerable, or open to harm. Cobras may seem like tough predators, but they need humans to look out for them too.

FATAL FACTS

A small **mammal** called a mongoose can kill cobras. The mongoose is quick and can dodge the cobra. The mongoose's thick coat makes it hard for cobras to deliver their venomous bite.

In many countries, including China and Vietnam, the king cobra is a protected species.

GLOSSARY

defense: a way of guarding against an enemy

digest: to break down food inside the body so that the body can use it

endangered: in danger of dying out

expert: someone with great knowledge about a certain subject

habitat: the natural place where an animal or plant lives

inject: to use sharp teeth to force venom into an animal's body

mammal: a warm-blooded animal that has a backbone and hair, breathes air, and feeds milk to its young

organ: a part inside an animal's body

pierce: to make a hole through

prey: an animal hunted by other animals for food

region: a large area of land that has features that make it different from nearby areas of land

slither: to slide easily over the ground

venom: something an animal makes in its body that can harm other animals

vibration: a rapid movement back and forth

FOR MORE INFORMATION

Books

Boutland, Craig. *King Cobra.* Minneapolis, MN: Bearport Publishing Company, 2021.

Pallotta, Jerry. *Komodo Dragon vs. King Cobra (Who Would Win?).* New York, NY: Scholastic, 2016.

Websites

Cobra

animals.sandiegozoo.org/animals/cobra

Find out more details about the cobra on this website.

King Cobra

kids.nationalgeographic.com/animals/reptiles/facts/king-cobra

Watch a quick video and discover more fun facts about the cobra here.

INDEX